North Star

Chiara Laricchiuta

AOS PUBLISHING, 2024

AOS POETRY, 2024

ISBN: 978-1-990496-28-8

Cover Design: Antonietta D'Amore

Visit AOS Publishing's website:
www.aospublishing.com

I dedicate this special collection to my daughter, Valesca, whose tender heart, magnetic charm and invigorating energy follow me everywhere I go. This collection is sprinkled with stardust, that very dust that you are made of, Valesca. Your incredible talents and hardworking nature inspire me. I am so proud to be your mother. You have taught me so much about myself, and about the power of maternal love. You have made me a better person. I love you profoundly.

I also dedicate this collection to everyone who has a dream, one they hold very close to their heart. One that perhaps has been left and revisited like a lost love, but that is so inextricably woven into the fabric of your soul, that it is impossible to extinguish or ignore. Maybe it is a dream that has never been uttered, for it is too precious to share or perhaps it has already taken incredible flight. Wherever you are on your journey, my hope is to instill in all my readers, innocent and wise alike, the hope, the courage, and the passion to continue believing and reaching for those bright stars that are shining in the infinite sky of dreams. Each star holds a distinct dream, for each and every one of us who truly believes.

Acknowledgments

I would like to thank AOS publishing for once again embracing my work. I am very grateful for your support.

To my husband, Anthony, who is always supportive and eager to embark on creative journeys with me, thank you sweetheart.

To my family, Love is everything, tutto il resto passa.

"The bold sky above reminds us that our dreams have a special place to live. The bright stars prove that our dreams can come true."

Table of Contents

Poems

Author's Note

North Star is my second collection of poetry. This collection is meant to spark a strong desire to tap into yourself and acknowledge the unique set of skills and talents that only you possess, and that are undeniably yours just like the sound of your voice. Believe in yourself and invest precious time, and you as well as those around you will relish in the priceless joy that comes from understanding your true purpose.

I've divided my collection into three chapters represented by a distinct color that holds a precious theme.

Red – red stars are some of the coolest stars in the universe. They are the oldest stars. Red represents the wise past that is our teacher.

White – white stars in our universe represent dying stars, or as I call them, spirit stars. White pays homage to our spirit self and those very special stars called our ancestors.

Blue – blue stars are the hottest, most massive, and the brightest stars of all. I call them dream stars. Blue represents dreams coming true.

The colors blue, red and white along with a bright yellow star appear on The Acadian Flag, which represents my birthplace of Bathurst, New Brunswick.

It is a very special place that I hold near and dear to my heart.

When I first thought of dividing my book into star-colored chapters, I had not realized the important meaning I was about to unravel.

This is a testament to the true magic of the universe.

RED (heart)

Like a burning heart, like a star beating and pulsating with LOVE and PASSION.

A Love Letter from Me to You

Nothing is the same without you.

You weren't supposed to go. I want you back.

I want you here next to me, but then I worry about how it would be.

Now that you are gone it is hard to feel happy and safe.

My heart is broken again. How many times did you break my heart?

I lost count. It doesn't matter.

Sometimes before going to sleep, my anxiety shifts to over-drive, because I wonder where you have gone and if you are okay.

I still worry about you. Does that make sense?

I am very pleased when you come to me in my dreams,

I get to feel you close to me once more.

I can speak freely about so many things, get to know you again, tell you things that you didn't know about me, learn things I didn't know about you.

I want to hug you, the way we used to.

I want you to know I will carry you with me for as long as I live.

I miss you. I love you. I forgive you for everything.

Please find this letter, it is a love letter from me to you.

An Undesired Pause

You came into the night and stole my senses.
I trembled like a thousand winters were upon me.
My body fought to be rescued from such a wretched state.
You left me aching and sulky like my tasteless tongue.
Quarantined like a shunned leper, confined to a room, the
only thing I could smell was fear all around me.
You may have interrupted my blissful path like a rude, ruthless
criminal but never could you alter my spirit and my deep
yearning to create.

Autumn Dance

Folded in half, an uncomfortable stance.
On bended knee, proposing a desired transformation.
Dipped down low in a valley of hope, wreathed in soil.
Dancing in the wind, uncovering a hidden truth,
mystical colors permeated in the foliage, exuding courage:
deep crimson, mustard seed, sunburst orange.
The season is changing, the dance is slower, but more refined.
The compass points to magnetic North.
In unison, the pines wave goodbye.

Cara Fragola,

Non aver paura dei sentimenti che provi,
è difficile da credere ma guariranno, ti lasceranno, l'amore è
troppo forte.
Toccalo con la passione furiosa che è dentro di te, vuole
sentire il tuo calore.
Parlagli con le parole che sai che vuole sentire, è la tua voce
che desidera.
Quella voce che lo riporta a un tempo più felice e più
semplice.
Abbraccialo con l'abbandono che provi, vuole sentire il tuo
amore.
Non è che un uomo mortale, desideroso di essere salvato dal
tuo perdono.

Castle in the Sky

Your words never broke me, they made me stronger.
You thought you could crush my spirit, I shined brighter.
I swallowed your lies and spit out butterflies.
I read your predictable mind and created art.
You tried to steal my heart and I gave birth to my own castle in
the sky.

Disconnecting

All around me there is sadness.
I look up and see the clouds engulfed in heavy tears.
The storm of grief has swept through my heart and into the
sky.

I turn to the brown sparrow in the tree.
He stares back at me silently refraining from singing his joyous
tune,
He is as still as the night.

The earth is damp and cold.
It reminds me that your body has turned to stone.
All that is left are memories of yesterdays gone by
and the curse of loneliness on my skin.

Earth Goat

Once upon a time, there lived a kind, little goat
Who felt different from the rest, so she wrote.
When things went wrong,
She tried to write a song,
Some days her feelings were so mixed,
All she wanted to do was cry until everything got fixed.
Weeping all day wasn't her cup of tea,
but writing things down helped her understand,
what she was destined to see.
Her songbook got thicker year after year.
More pages with words, messages, and meanings.
To think, this one magical book had helped manage,
all her strong feelings.
The same question kept arising,
making her blush like a rose,
Perhaps sharing my stories,
could help others with their woes?

Fires

He lied and
I died.
I had nowhere to hide.
I tried to
pick up the pieces,
but
the
dark, crimson blood in my veins
was too,
thick and hot
to be bothered.
So, I burned everything,
in my path,
until all I saw
were ashes,
all around me.
Maybe it was
foreshadowing
for when
he actually
died
and
I
Survived
Another
Fire.

Fragola

Don't be afraid of the feelings you feel.
It is hard to believe but they will heal. They will leave you. The love is too strong.
Touch him with the raging passion that's inside you. He wants to feel your warmth.
Speak to him with the words you know he wants to hear. It's your voice he yearns for,
that voice that takes him back to a happier, simpler time.
Hug him with the abandonment you feel. He wants to feel your love.
He is but a mortal man, longing to be saved by your forgiveness.

Grief

It lives on our skin.
We pour water on it, and hope it gently washes away.
When it returns unexpectedly, we try to scrape it off with more
aggressive strokes.
We think it will heal like an open wound we disinfect.
It is a stubborn stain. It does not go away.
As much as we want to remove it, it lives on our skin.

How Could it Be?

How could it be that you no longer exist?
If you witness day turn into night.
How could it be that your spirit has vanquished from this
place?
If I still smell your warm breath on my lips.
Is it right that I pretend your name is an unfamiliar sound?
When I know the melody of your voice is music to someone
else's heart.

Know Your Worth

You're nobody's half time show.
Stand up and take a bow.
No one gets to tell you what to do anymore.
You listened and you learned.
Now you can march to the beat of your own drum.
You know, you could run before you learned how to walk?
You always did things your own special way, you always
surprised us.
The pain never made you feel weak, you colored it with
burning red passion.
Your first word was mamma.

Parkwood Drive

Under an Acadian sunset
savoring the catch of the day,
brothers and fathers gather,
to celebrate a gift.

Mothers and daughters hold each other tight.
They share their hopes, they share their dreams.
The smell of love is in the air, as they marvel at the miracle of
life.
The Stella Maris is shining bright in the sky.

A long road traveled, a unique path retraced,
decades later, to relive a sweet moment in time.
To touch something special, taking it all in,
the beauty of the universe, things come full circle,
what joy it brings!

Shedding

Shedding the tears that smudged the glorious art.
Shedding the heavy weight that made it laborious to take a full breath.
Shedding the pain that engulfed the weary mind.
Shedding the thick layer of protective armor that made it tough to trust.
Clearing a space for all the love that exists.

Silent Fall

A bed of wet leaves,
Washing away the cold pain,
Making space for time.

Straight Shooter

Do I offend you?
I'm not trying to, I'm really not!
I'm just observing and decoding, trying to
find meaning in this chaotic stage of life.
We are all looking for something, some are racing, some are
taking their time,
It's not about the destination because we all know that is the
only democratic place we'll ever be. Isn't it ironic?
While we are headed there, might as well have fun, and laugh,
at all the ways we try to trick ourselves into believing that our
time will never come.
The things we do to occupy our time and space – all the
distractions that we choose. Maybe we should stop fearing *it*?
How does one do that you ask?
Perhaps by asking lots of questions and trying to find answers
that will lead to other questions. Does that sound insane? One
WO-man's meat is another WO-man's poison.
Maybe it's all in the here and now, living in the spectacular
now as imperfect as it may be.
It is the only thing that really exists. Why bother worrying
about anything else?

I'm just trying to provoke raw emotions in a time when
emotions have been *numbified* by digital illusions and artificial
intelligence. We take pills to get rid of them, instead of looking
in the mirror and dealing, we paint the sadness with color that
washes away. And then we wonder, where all the unhappiness
comes from? Clearly, it's just easier surviving in perpetual
denial.

The Child Within

Hello long lost friend.
How are you?
It's been so long.
Just checking in.
Did all your dreams come true?
Where did you wander to find YOUR path?
Did you ever find true love?
Wondering how you think you've done so far?
Hope you never lost that special inner spark!

The Sword

Who writes the laws and starts the wars?
We cover up their wounds and disinfect the blame.
Who invades our space and abuses the disenfranchised mind?
We embrace the pain and pick up the pieces of shattered glass.
It slices us. We bleed. It stops momentarily through the silent
echoes of fleeting disingenuous confessions. Another fruitless
cycle is born.
Who craves the power and the fame?
We teach, we share, we cultivate hope.
They try to slay us but LOVE never dies.

The Trinity of My Heart

Three sisters united in love, united in pain.
United in ways there is abundant wisdom to gain.
Three tender souls, sharing dreams, dispelling fears.
Honoring differences and washing away tears.
Three sweet spirits locked into one heart,
each carrying a special light,
Exalting, what makes them shine bright.
Three sisters forever linked by lineage,
bonded by the blessing of being friends.

Traveling Gypsies

Tons of bags, different shapes and sizes marked by years spent embarking on journeys – some long, others short, but always meaningful.

Foreign dialects always pleasing to meet, as charming as old country songs.

Chests filled with trinkets and photographs.

Never feeling like you really belong, wrapped up in a hybrid of love and fear.

Following an unknown path carved and wedged by another man's dreams.

Is it destiny? Is this the sky I was meant to be praying under tonight?

The sun rises in a new place, and you nevertheless emerge with budding confidence.

What's in a Name?

Combined letters to form an extraordinary word.
A personal tag to acknowledge your place in the universe.
Chosen by someone special.
Passed down to you, so you, could shine and share your
distinct history.
Before your journey began, someone cared.
Someone was hoping all your dreams would come true.
If this does not make you dream bigger, and hope deeper, I'm
not sure what will.

WHITE (peace)

White, peace, like the star connecting you to your spirit-self and your ancestors who are applauding you and your dreams.

Ancestral Bond

I see you in the monarch butterfly fluttering in the summer breeze,
ensuring the garden is well, smiling at the sacred space you passed down.
You are the ladybug that is always around me, making me smile and wonder.
I saw you at the park last week, you landed on my shoulder flaunting your love.
The maple bursting through the fertile earth, reminiscent of your strength. The long branches that extend wide like your generosity that knew no bounds.
Your face is in the clouds. Some days I can see it so clearly.
Your magnetic energy is part of the sun. It comforts me like those warm fires you would start.
I hear the wind carrying your unforgettable voice, it reminds me that we are still together.
You will always be around me because I believe you are there.
You are shining brightly in the starry sky, in fact, you are the brightest star.
I know you want me to recognize you even when you are hidden, to honor you, to remember you.
That is why you follow me everywhere I go.

Cathedral Bells

The clanging of the old church bells, reminding us that there is
something more important above.

We can hear them, but we ignore them, like the poor, needy
beggar in rags ruining the pretty scene.

Hastily we buy gifts and sprint to the local market, our carts
spilling with seasonal delights.

The soup kitchen down by the old brewery looks like a ghost
town.

Not a soul has bothered to make a stop, it would spoil the
festive fun.

"The spirit of giving is upon us," calls out the tall man on the
megaphone, "We should keep the magic alive."

A young child tugs on his mother's coat and whispers, "I've
asked Santa for a toy train this year."

On the holiest of nights, we marvel at the colorful lights. We
gather by the fire eating toasty chestnuts. We sing some classic
carols.

While the forgotten ones cry themselves to sleep to the sound
of the Cathedral bells.

D'Amore

An exclusive design,
Never on sale,
Premium quality,
Intricate detail,
Meticulously curated,
Authentically made in Italy,
With unconditional love.

D'Amore (In Italiano)

Un design esclusivo,
Mai in vendita,
Qualità premium,
Dettagli intricati,
Curato meticolosamente,
Autenticamente made in Italy,
Con amore incondizionato.

Every Shoe Tells a Story

Tiny slippers – delicate and pure – seeking love and care.
White sneakers – running towards adventure, fearless, full of
vitality, invincibility at the helm partnered with enthusiasm and
energy.
Red rain boots – combating the trenches, making sense of the
mission, the existentialist crisis is real.
Black loafers – worn for comfort and security, necessitating
calm and peace, enjoying what's left of the party.
Barefoot and naked – ready to let go.

Warning: wear the shoes that fit at the right time.
If they are not comfortable don't try to break them in!

Five Rocks

Five rocks, standing firmly, one fully submerged, the others still
above water.
A flowing river, the rustling of damp autumn leaves, losing
their luster in the cold earth.
The smell of wood burning, rehashing recollections,
extinguishing all the fear.

Understanding the merriment that comes from abandoning
frivolous desires.
Welcoming the change fuelling from within, honoring the
voice that seeks serenity.
Uniquely found in the here and now.

The wind carrying the momentum and courage to howl the
divine truth that nothing lasts.
The calm resignation exhibited by the naked trees, vulnerable
but not frail.
We open our hearts to the wisdom; we surrender to its
immutable force.

Holy Healing

Planting seeds of optimism, that will sprout when you need them most.
Trusting that the universe will manifest special miracles just for you.
Treating nature as your muse.
Relying on your innate intelligence guiding you home to your true self.

Legame Ancestrale

Ti vedo nella farfalla monarca che svolazza nella brezza estiva,
Assicurando che il giardino stia bene, sorridendo allo spazio
sacro che viene tramandato.
Sei la coccinella che è sempre intorno a me, facendomi
sorridere e meravigliare.
Ti ho visto al parco la scorsa settimana, sei atterrato sulla mia
spalla ostentando il tuo amore.
L'acero che irrompe nella terra fertile, che ricorda la tua forza,
i lunghi rami che si estendono larghi come la tua generosità
che non conosceva limiti.
Il tuo viso è tra le nuvole, alcuni giorni posso vederlo così
chiaramente.
La tua energia magnetica fa parte del sole, mi conforta come
quei fuochi caldi che avresti acceso.
Sento il vento portare la tua voce indimenticabile, mi ricorda
che siamo ancora insieme.
Sarai sempre intorno a me perché credo che ci sei.
Brilli brillantemente nel cielo stellato, infatti, sei la stella più
luminosa.
So che vuoi essere riconoscuito anche quando sei nascosto,
per onorarti, per ricordarti,
Ecco perché mi segui ovunque io vada.

Paradoxical Footprints

Magnetic energy,
Infectious resonance,
Stinging utterances used to anecdote life,
Omniscient point of view,
Aware of thy worth,
Crusader of the marginalized,
Born to flourish.

Reflections

Windows to the soul,
Wise and deeply intuitive like an ocean, blue.
Bright and as natural as the woodland, green.
Reliable and grounded like the earth, brown.
Formal and as enigmatic as a timeless work of art, black.
A looking glass, reflecting flowing phases and impediments.
They take you on a journey, one of self-discovery,
of profound meaning and connection,
as intimate as your last breath.

Sugar Coated

I see you so clearly, your taste is so familiar.
It is layered with a subtle flavor that only my palette can detect.
Your bitter-sweet aura, whipped in mystery, I can easily unravel.
Your half smile, sprinkled with superstition and pain.
Extra toppings to add to your luxurious blend of pleasure.
The long-lasting satisfaction – the craving always fulfilled.

The Divine

Like a prayer calling your name,
Anointed with a solemn grace,
As pure as a guardian angel protecting a beloved soul,
A spiritual epiphany casting shadows on the doubts that have
stifled your emancipation.
The savior within revealed and honored for the beauty it holds.
You have touched the deepest part of yourself,
That is where God resides.

Wise One

Ancient eyes that sparkle with such otherworldly knowledge.
You came to me again in my dreams.
You stood there beaming until I noticed you.
I was honored to see you again and share my sacred space.
You seemed so happy, strong, and confident,
just as I remember you.
You hugged me and you spread your joy so selflessly.
You comforted me like a warm sunny day.
You helped me regain my energy and touch the divinity in your
eyes.

BLUE (freedom)

Like the freedom you deserve, like the faith and confidence you must find in yourself to unleash the inspiration to make all of your dreams come true.

Awakening

A sanguine thirst quenched by an overflowing glass of colorful dreams.
An anchor of pain unclenched by the caress of a silent bow coming from the inner voice of your soul.
Electricity sparking through your body, nourishing it with buzzing creative energy.
The sun warming your heart with the courage to forgive.
A river of kindness spilling in every direction you turn.
Love navigating the vessel of life.

BIG Energy

You feel that big energy?
It feels like love at first sight.
It gives you the momentum you need to pursue your biggest dream.
It fills you with joy and inspiration.
It's the mystery of the universe smiling at you.
Congratulating you for having turned one blossom,
into a magnificent botanical garden of gold, lavender, and emerald flowers, for everyone to enjoy.
Every day the garden flourishes and radiates with love and freedom to grow stronger,
Your kind gestures never go unnoticed, your gifts are well received.
Your deep connection to the world around you will leave an eternal legacy.

BIG Ideas

Universal connections
Cosmic forces
The interrelated wonder of being alive.
We are part of the bold sky of dreams. We are the sky of
dreams.
We hold precious seeds inside our hearts.
Seeds that will blossom at the very moment, that we need them
most.
Those seeds are filled with all the manifestations we have been
cultivating from the day we were born.

Bold Sky

A canvas of stars,
Phases of high energy,
Cascading bright dreams.

Crusader of the Light

Have the winds of change altered your gaze?
Have you replaced the hummingbird's tune with the buzzing
distraction in your mental maze?
It's time to dig deep, get calm, don't weep.
Seek the tender hand of a sister, of a friend,
good advice and wisdom, she can lend.
It's ok to feel down, don't let yourself drown.
You are too precious, you are too rare,
Your dreams are important, dare to care.
For you alone are enough, you are what matters.
Only you can steer, the natural movement of your light,
And determine when the time is right,
To wear your crown of personal sovereignty.

Cut, Paste and Color

Cut around what no longer serves you – keep the best parts, the ones that make you stronger. Be proud of them!

Paste – add the sprinkles and glitter that make it uniquely yours. All the nuances that could only belong to you. Make it shine!

Color your canvas with all the dreams and passion you've got – it's your creation it deserves to be seen and felt. Share it!

Dolce Far Niente

Pondering happily on a quiet Saturday evening,
A cup of warm soothing cider, perhaps another, keeping you in
sweet company.
Time stands still under a blanket of cherished memories.
Softly turning the pages cf a dusty paperback, the one that's
been burning for your affection.
Listening to the delicate pitter-patter of the rain, with no
destination in sight.
The clarity of what matters is right in front of you, you are
bathing in your ocean of peace.

Falling Star

I would sit under the moonlit sky and pray.
I would pray until the angels came to me.
They softly carried away my fears on their delicate wings and
whispered, "We are here."
I would sit under the moonlit sky and sing,
I would sing until I heard the soft echo of a voice.
The voice was soft and clear, "They are near."
I would sit under the moonlit sky and wish.
I would wish until one day I met my dreams.
They held my hand and said, "We have been waiting for you.
You found us."

Instruments of Time

The flute,
plays a joyful tune, recalling a time of relentless energy and
vigor.
The violin,
echoes sorrow and melancholy that reminds us of the fragility of
life.
The guitar,
strums powerful patterns and revives the great strength within all
of us.
The piano,
tickles a timeless sonata that pays homage to all the great loves
in our lives.
The drums,
beat deeply into our hearts and touch that which awakens our
spirit.

La Canzone del Mare

She sat there silently in deep thought,
While the warm summer breeze gently brushed her golden
locks streaked in nostalgia.
The ocean began singing a soft sonata,
Taking her back to all her sweet yesterdays.
In that moment, she relived love stories and quiet realizations.
Her old sorrows returned to her, but she had met them all
before,
They weren't strangers anymore.
They wouldn't turn into tomorrow's fears.
This delicate miracle gave birth to an endless stream of tears.
She swallowed them whole,
As they brought her closer to the sun.

La Canzone del Mare (In Italiano)

Seduta in silenzio in profonda riflessione,
Mentre la tiepida brezza estiva sfiorava dolcemente i suoi
riccioli dorati striati di nostalgia.
L'oceano cominciò a cantare una dolce sonata,
Riportandola a tutti i suoi dolci ieri.
In quel momento, ha rivissuto storie d'amore e realizzazioni
tranquille.
I suoi vecchi dolori tornarono, ma li aveva incontrati tutti prima.
Non erano più estranei.
Non si trasformerebbero nelle paure di domani.
Questo delicato miracolo ha dato vita a un flusso infinito di
lacrime.
Li ha inghiottiti interi,
Mentre la avvicinavano al sole.

Love

Love is in the natural beauty all around us.
Love is learning about yourself.
Love is telling yourself; I love you.
Love is watching people grow.
Love is freedom, the freedom and space you graciously give
yourself and everyone you encounter to be who they are.
Love is knowing that because you exist someone else has an
opportunity to love.

Manifestations

Ideas that turned into words.
Words that ignited ambition.
Ambition that awoke desires.
Desires that became vivid dreams.
Dreams that transformed into truth.
Truth that brings everlasting bliss.

Ode to Valesca

I've got rhythm, I've got rhyme.
I've got plenty of sunshine.
When I'm down, I don't frown.
I just get up and fix my crown.

I've got spirit, I've got love,
that guides me from above.
I am strong, I am real.
I know exactly how I feel.

I work hard and put in time,
someday soon, I will climb.
And reach the stars I've been searching for,
where all my dreams will soar.

Quill

I look for you when I am down.
You help me sort things out, to release what,
I long to part with,
And to share what I want to pass along.
You help me create magic from despair.
You turn my fears into dreams,
that color my heart.

Retroactive Compensation

Is there a leprechaun waiting over the rainbow with a big pot of gold?
Is Santa keeping tabs on how many times you made the nice list?
Maybe Jesus is checking to see if you are turning the other cheek?
Endless pleases and thank-yous.
Sharing comforting smiles.
Random acts of altruism.
You don't need the accolades; you don't need the glory of recognition.
The prize is the upward climb – knowing you've done the hard work and
reached the top all by yourself!

Risveglio

Una sete sanguigna placata da un bicchiere traboccante di sogni colorati,
Un'ancora di dolore sbloccata dalla carezza di un arco silenzioso proveniente dalla voce interiore della tua anima.
Elettricità che scintilla attraverso il tuo corpo, nutrendolo con un'energia creativa ronzante.
Il sole che scalda il tuo cuore con il coraggio di perdonare
Un fiume di gentilezza che si riversa in ogni direzione in cui giri.
Amore che naviga nel vascello della vita.

Seasons

Every season has a reason,
To teach us lessons and embrace our blessings.
To remind us to treat others just like we would our brothers.
To show we care and begin to share,
Our wisdom, our light, our love.
Planting seeds of hope,
Saying I am sorry, saying I forgive you.
Meditating on the words, thank you and I love you every day.

Star Story

Home is where your heart resides, sitting closely next to mine.
Beating to a soft tune, believing everything is fine.
Glowing with light and warming with care,
Always open with something to share.
Discovering truths and transforming pain.
Beautifully interconnected with imperfect balance.
Seeking enlightenment at no time in vain.

Sublime

The hope that radiates from one candle,
can light up the night,
and give the stars the courage,
to sing a symphony in the sky.

Sweet Love

Being with you sets me free.
For with you, I can be the authentic me.
You lift my spirits when I am down,
Open my mind to things I can't always see.
Joy and laughter you bring to my heart
I can't ever imagine us apart.
Through the rain and storms,
We are stronger together.
My lover, my best friend.
I love us.
I love you, sweetheart!

Swimming in Honey

Creating waves of thick golden amber,
sweetness all around you.
Splashing kindness in your every stroke.
Embracing people for who they are and want to be.
Floating in a soothing bath releasing all the chains that have kept
you from reaching your true north.
Taking in deep gulps of humility and spitting out the excess, the
false pretenses that don't serve you.
You just created your own pot of gold.

Synchronicity

Awe-inspiring experiences, designed by time.
A culmination of coming together.
Releasing fruitless patterns.
Propelling forward with courage and confidence.
Observing the righteous path is in reach.
Touching the divinity within.
Carving an incredible truth.
Meeting a twin flame.
Detaching from the material world.
Letting the ego die.

The Third Eye

Noticing all the signs, senses are heightened.
Incongruences leave you unshaken.
Resilience and trust deeply rooted in your divine inner strength.
Guided by an ancestral providence that steers your life stream.
Into the direction of your most precious dream.

Taking an Inward Turn in an Age of Virtual Excess

What do human beings want most? What is it that we collectively desire: Is it love? Is it peace? Is it health or wealth? Is it the impossible dream of immortality? Perhaps it's a colorful medley of all these things wrapped up in a big golden bow called freedom and self-realization.

How are we supposed to make the best of the time we have here on this planet so that when we are faced with the inevitable, eternal slumber, we feel full of life? Synonymous to the feeling of satisfaction that arises after having thoroughly enjoyed a delicious meal or better still the fulfillment that comes from having accomplished everything on our sacred to do list.

A good point of departure would be to reflect upon how we use our time. Are we using it resourcefully? Are we finding work/life/family balance? Are we finding spiritual time to be the best versions of ourselves? These questions make me want to eat chocolate and binge-watch my favorite Netflix series again! Escapism and procrastination are much more entertaining than dwelling in the here and now of hard work. Alas, there is always a high cost to pay for indulging.

Technology and social media have given us the perfect excuses to numb reality. For many of us, they have become ever so comfortable and convenient gap fillers. The "extra time" we have at our disposal is spent on our digital poison of choice: Facebook, Instagram, Netflix. We occupy so much of our *spare* time invested in the virtual world that we are forgetting how to live in the real one. The empty illusion of instant gratification and public opinion consuming our extra minutes, adds up to a quality-of-life deficit. Think about it: has the superfluous culture of social exposure really been a healthy social movement? Has it cultivated togetherness, or has it ironically perpetuated unwanted feelings of depression, anxiety, and insecurity in our youth? The tragic misconception of feeling connected has ultimately created an army of digital addicts, frantically worried about what we are going to miss or forget to like or endorse, while neglecting our real relationships and live moments that are streaming for a limited time only.

We procrastinate with the arrogant conviction that time will stand still for us or that there will come a better time to do such and such a thing. The sad and obvious newsflash that we tend to mute is that the time to do, to act, to love and to forgive is right now. There is no better time to live in the real world.

Detoxing from the frenzy of technology, might create the happier, healthier balance we seek and provide a clearer understanding of where our priorities lie when it comes to caring for our "extra time".

Above all, it will teach our children that they are worth much more than a like and that there is so much more life to look forward to other than the illusive gratification that an instant message provides. Over the past 16 years teaching college English, I have had the privilege of meeting and teaching some of the wonderful members of our future generation. However, what I have sadly observed over time is that our youth is finding it disconcerting to talk about themselves and their future. When I ask them what their skills are, some of them look at me with a mortified hazy expression, until the desolate words "I don't know" are uttered. This was not the case when I first began teaching 16 years ago. Why is it so different? Perhaps because some of the 18-year-olds today have been born into the crushing clutch of technology and social media from day one.

It should not bewilder us when we discover that they feel lost and alone. The excess of the virtual world has infiltrated so many aspects of their young lives that they are not sure about what they want and how they will materialize their real goals.

They need more guidance and support than ever and as responsible adults and caregivers it is our responsibility to do our part.

Being alive and fully aware of our potential and skills is a beautiful thing, an irreplaceable gift wrapped up in a shiny red bow called Love. Something that we should all be invested in. We should check into that self-rehab from technology overload today to make more quality time for what really matters.

About the Author

Chiara Laricchiuta was born in Bathurst, New Brunswick and was raised by Italian immigrant parents in Montreal, Canada. She is a proud Canadian with very strong roots in her Italian culture. She is a college professor in Montreal, Canada. She has been teaching English for over 16 years. She has an undergraduate degree in English Literature from McGill University. She also has a graduate certificate in T.E.S.L from McGill University. In 2009, she obtained a Master's in Educational Studies from Concordia University. In addition to teaching, she has been writing creatively for over 20 years. Writing has always been her passion. In 2004, she completed a certificate in Journalism at Concordia University and began publishing her work in *The Bridge Magazine*, a magazine for new students at Concordia. Since then, some of her creative pieces have been published in magazines such as *Accenti Magazine,* a cultural magazine highlighting the uniqueness of the Italian Canadian experience in Montreal.

Her first collection of poetry entitled "Recollections of My Soul" was published in July 2023 by AOS Publishing.
When she isn't teaching or writing, Chiara loves to travel to Southern Italy and spends all her free time with her husband and young daughter.